Benjamin Ide Wheeler

Dionysos and Immortality

The Greek Faith in Immortality

Benjamin Ide Wheeler

Dionysos and Immortality
The Greek Faith in Immortality

ISBN/EAN: 9783743367067

Manufactured in Europe, USA, Canada, Australia, Japa

Cover: Foto ©ninafisch / pixelio.de

Manufactured and distributed by brebook publishing software
(www.brebook.com)

Benjamin Ide Wheeler

Dionysos and Immortality

DIONYSOS
AND IMMORTALITY

THE GREEK FAITH IN
IMMORTALITY AS AFFECTED BY THE
RISE OF INDIVIDUALISM

BY

BENJAMIN IDE WHEELER

PRESIDENT OF THE UNIVERSITY OF CALIFORNIA
AND INGERSOLL LECTURER FOR 1898–99

BOSTON AND NEW YORK
HOUGHTON, MIFFLIN AND COMPANY
The Riverside Press, Cambridge
1899

THE INGERSOLL LECTURESHIP

Extract from the will of Miss Caroline Haskell Ingersoll, who died in Keene, County of Cheshire, New Hampshire, Jan. 26, 1893.

First. In carrying out the wishes of my late beloved father, George Goldthwait Ingersoll, as declared by him in his last will and testament, I give and bequeath to Harvard University in Cambridge, Mass., where my late father was graduated, and which he always held in love and honor, the sum of Five thousand dollars ($5,000) as a fund for the establishment of a Lectureship on a plan somewhat similar to that of the Dudleian lecture, that is — one lecture to be delivered each year, on any convenient day between the last day of May and the first day of December, on this subject, "the Immortality of Man," said lecture not to form a part of the usual college course, nor to be delivered by any Professor or Tutor as part of his usual routine of instruction, though any such Professor or Tutor may be appointed to such service. The choice of said lecturer is not to be limited to any one religious denomination, nor to any one profession, but may be that of either clergyman or layman, the appointment to take place at least six months before the delivery of said lecture. The above sum to be safely invested and three fourths of the annual interest thereof to be paid to the lecturer for his services and the remaining fourth to be expended in the publishment and gratuitous distribution of the lecture, a copy of which is always to be furnished by the lecturer for such purpose. The same lecture to be named and known as "the Ingersoll lecture on the Immortality of Man."

DIONYSOS AND IMMORTALITY

NO people has ever possessed a religion more delicately responsive to its moods than the people of ancient Greece. This they owed in large measure to the absence of an ecclesiastical organization. The Greek instinctively abhorred all mechanism, for mechanism, as guaranteeing like and constant output to like time and like material, ignored free personality, — and this free personality was to the Greek the one recognized source of all creative movement. Least of all did he need the ecclesiastical machine. There was no priestly hierarchy either for Greece as a whole or for single cantons; not even among priests of the same cult in different cantons was there organized coöperation. Some popular shrine or oracle might win more than ' local prestige and secure the protection and support of various neighboring states, but *there* the drift toward centralization and organization found its limit.

At no time did there exist an organized authority which could formulate standards of faith or dictate the usages of religious etiquette. Ritual, seeking that which in matter and manner was believed to be well pleasing to the gods, followed the traditions of the individual shrines, and there were no better theologians than the poets. Dogmas there were none. In contrast with the religious experience of a land like India, Greece stands at the extreme. There religion was imposed as a system from without, here it sprang as a social and civic impulse from within.

This fundamental characteristic endows the study of Greek religious thought at once with singular charm and with singular difficulty. We know on the one hand that if we can penetrate through the thick-tangled meshes of mythology and ritual to the unspoken faiths lying behind, we shall find them hard by the life conditions and the views of life which were their source. On the other hand, as no authority essayed to formulate what Greeks *should* believe, so no contemporary was moved to state in connected form, nor presumably even to think, what they *did* believe.

Research has spent itself in following the shifting forms of the mythology through glade, and fen, and grotto, until they prove themselves most mere will-o'-the-wisps, — light-winged fancies, whether of poets who write, or of poets who dream and write not. Sometimes they are mirror flashes from the ritual thrown upon the valley mist, sometimes they are dim ghosts of a storied past, sometimes they are shadowy images of nature and her signs, but seldom are they trusty guides into the land of reality. Other guides we must follow if we would come to a knowledge of the plain faith by which men stayed their lives, measured their duty, estimated the meaning of life's beginning and life's end.

I propose in what follows to speak of one phase of this plain, inner faith among the Greeks, the belief in the life after death, and, lest I wander too far afield, to speak in particular of the marvelous quickening and development which that belief underwent during one most significant epoch in the national life. It is in its readjustment to changed conditions of life and new views of the world that a people's faith best betrays whither its face is really set. That which conditions it then becomes the background against which we measure it.

In undertaking this task we do not shut our eyes to the fact that in Old Greece there were, as now, many men and many minds, — that there was diversity in the beliefs of different tribes and districts, that there were strongly marked strata of intelligence or culture, that survivals from earlier horizons of belief, be it through the forms of ritual or through the revered texts of the national epic, continually intruded themselves to confuse the bearings in the new, but still there is a law in things human that that which holds itself below the attacks of systematic reason tends toward homogeneity and unity, — and Greece in the period with which we deal had not yet fallen ill of philosophy.

As part of the common stock of primitive human thought the Greek inherited the natural consciousness for being as absolute, as unbounded by non-being. To forget is the one gate of annulment. The common human belief in the shadowy second-self, revealed, it may well be, in the experiences of sleep and dreams, swoons and ecstasies, was also his belief, and to him man was body and soul.

When a man dies, the soul issues forth from the body to seek other residence. And not man's life alone is thus dual; all life, of beast, of tree, of the river current, of the fountain, of the wind and the storm-cloud, is made up of body and soul. For the primitive Greek as for the primitive man, there was no other way in which to think of life.

Even philosophy when it made its first attempts began in terms of this same simple dualism which dominated all thought, and the ἀρχή, water, air, or fire, which Thales, Anaximenes, and Herakleitos inquired after, was conceived in the analogy of the ψυχή; it was the world-soul.

If we are to believe, as it seems likely we must, that the religion of primitive man [1] received its character in the struggle to conciliate and be at peace with soul-life dwelling and wandering in his environment, then we can say that the primitive Greek religion, or, if we dare use the term, the Indo-European religion,[2] had made so much advance upon this, that it had introduced certain classifications, a certain system and order, certain limitations into the chaos of soul-dreads and soul-worships. It had developed the family, the greater family or clan, and the tribe as definite organizations existing for the purpose, or held together by the usage, of caring for the souls of ancestors, the family the nearer, the tribe the remoter. It had restricted the care for spirits resident in natural objects mostly to specific cults and shrines, and through generalization upon natural objects and phenomena had obtained certain types of the so-called, " nature-gods." Nature-gods as such, however, there were none.

Between soul-worship and nature-worship, at least from the point of view of Greek religion, no sharp line of demarcation is to be drawn. The primitive belief in the residence of souls in natural objects colored all the later developments of the theogony, and the great gods, the " nature-gods," carried up with them from their origin the semblances of ancestor-gods, and as such always had the character of persons, members of the community, first citizens of tribe or state.

Thus Hermes, who always bears in his character suggestions of the phenomena of the wind, and develops attributes determined by the impression which these phenomena make upon the minds of men, is a fellow-citizen, an honorary member of the state-guild, an embodiment of the purpose and meaning of society and the state. Respect for him is a constituent part of loyalty; impiety toward him and his kind is treason, and treason has no other definition than impiety.

After the analogies of ancestor-worship kings traced their descent back to these gods, who were thus joined by the genealogies to the fate and fabric of the state. The gods, too, were related among themselves, and their organization into a bond of relationship gave color to the instinct of unity among the diverse tribes who owned them as kin. One of them bore, indeed, from Indo-European times, the title of "father" (Ζεῦ πάτερ, Jūpiter), and he remained in his character as father the personal sponsor for Hellenic unity.

All the observances of the ritual took their form from the primitive usages of feeding and entertaining souls. The feast for the dead, at which in the inner circle of the family the soul of the departed was esteemed the guest of honor, differed in substance no whit from the great sacrifices which the state offered its great gods. The funeral games for Patroklos were of the same significance as those offered for entertainment of Zeus in the plain of Olympia.

Throughout the whole life and practice of Greek religion the festivals retained the scantly disguised form of entertainments in honor of the gods as "first citizens" of the state, the tribe, or the association. The sacrifices were feasts at which the god and his entertainers dined together and partook of the same food, if not of the same life. The priests were the specialists in divine etiquette who knew what portions and what manners were pleasing to the personages who were the guests of honor. The games were an entertainment offered to the guests which were as certainly believed to be gratifying to their sight as a review of troops or a deer-hunt to a modern European sovereign.

To return now to our characterization of primitive, *i. e.*, præ-Homeric Greek religion,[3] we know that it maintained a system of offerings to the souls of the departed, and that these offerings were made at the graves where the souls were believed to linger, or to which on occasions they were wont to return. They were offerings of food, in which the offering of blood played a prominent part, and were intended to appease and conciliate the souls [4] and prevent the baneful intrusion of their wrath into the life of living men.

A belief in a place beneath the earth, a deep cavernous abode where all the souls were assembled, not for punishment or blessing, but simply for residence, was a part of the earliest faith, apparently derived from præ-Greek, probably Indo-European faith. The Vedic idea of a residence for the fathers in the heaven above the earth is, as Oldenberg [5] has made almost certain, a substitute for an earlier belief in an abode beneath the earth. In the Indo-

Iranian beliefs which lie behind the separate Indian and Iranian religions the dead were, as he seems to have demonstrated, conceived of as residing in the earth, and in conformity to this view the cult of the dead was originally celebrated. To induce the soul to retire into this common abode of the dead and there find contented rest is apparently the supreme aim and purpose of the rites of the grave among the early Hindoos as among the early Greeks.

In marked contrast now with this early faith and practice, which we have thus far been considering, the religion represented in the Homeric poems discovers an almost complete atrophy of the cultus of the dead. Once "the life-energy had left the white bones"[6] and the funeral pyre with its "stout force of gleaming fire o'ermastered" flesh and bones, then the psyche "flitting off like a dream is flown" to the "asphodel moors" beyond the river.

There it tarries in a shadowy existence without memory or will, and without interest in the affairs of men, or power to intrude itself into them. The recurring observances at the tomb had ceased. The feeding of souls and all the rites of soul-worship had been discontinued, for, after the soul had once been led by Hermes the guide down "the dank ways" and under "the misty gloom," it never retraced the path nor crossed the river again. Some strange wind of skepticism, some cold, clear *tramontana* of spiritual agnosticism, whose source and meaning we may never know, had purged of ghosts the air of Homer's world.[7] Proper burial was the one condition of purgation. So much at least lingered of the old.

As Achilles slept in the night after slaying Hector, the psyche of Patroklos, still free to wander about, while the body remained unburied, still possessed of reason and will, came and stood above Achilles' head, "altogether like to his very self, in stature, fair eyes, and voice, and like in the raiment he wore;" and spoke to him thus:

"So thou dost sleep, Achilles, but me thou hast forgotten. Not when I lived wast thou remiss, but now that I am dead. Make haste and bury me, that I may pass the gates of Hades. The spirits keep me wide aloof, these phantoms of the weary dead, nor suffer me to join with them beyond the river, and vainly do I roam around the wide-doored house of Hades. Nay, give me, I entreat of thee, thy hand, for nevermore shall I come back from Hades' land, when ye have paid me once my due of fire; and nevermore among the living shall we sit without the circle of our comrades and there take counsel with each other."[8]

The psyches, like vain shadows, "strengthless heads of the dead," reft of the *phrenes*, the organs of will and emotion,[9] flitted hither and thither without plan or purpose or hope. Thus at the close of Achilles' vision: "So spake he, and stretched out his hands but grasped him not, for vapor-like the spirit vanished into the ground with squeaking, gibbering cry. And in marvel sprung up

Achilles, and smiting his hands together uttered the word of woe, Ay me, verily then there is in the dwellings of Hades a spirit, a phantom, but *phrenes* it hath not at all."

And so after Odysseus has slain the suitors: "Cyllenian Hermes summoned together the shades of the suitors; and he held in his hands the wand that is golden and fair, wherewith he closes to sleep the eyes of whomsoever he will, while others he wakens from sleep. Therewith he started them forth and led them along, while they followed on with squeaking, gibbering cry. And just as when bats fly chirping about in the depth of some monstrous cave, and one has fallen from the cluster on the rock, and they cling fast one to the other, so they went on and chirped as they went, but Hermes the helper went on leading them down the dank ways, past the streams of Oceanus, past the White Rock, along by the gates of the Sun, past the parish of Dreams, till they come to the asphodel moor, where the spirits have their abode, the phantoms of way-worn men." [10]

The psyches are furthermore represented as without memory or the power of recognition, and in the Nekyia it is only through drinking the sacrificial blood from Odysseus' trench that these are restored to them.[11] "And I drew my sharp blade from my thigh and therewith dug a pit as much as a cubit this way and that. Around it I poured my libation for all the departed, first with the milk and the honey, then with sweet wine, and thirdly with water ; and over it barley-meal white I strewed."

Then the shades flocked about the trench, but Odysseus kept them off with his sword, waiting to catch sight of the seer Teiresias, who was the prime object of his search. Among them he saw the psyche of his mother ; "and I wept at sight of her and pitied her in my heart, but even so, sore grieved as I was I suffered her not to draw nigh to the blood, till I first had inquired of Teiresias."

Finally, after Odysseus had found the
seer and talked with him, he asks him how
he may bring his mother to recognize her
son: "I see the spirit here of my departed
mother; silent she sits beside the blood,
but has not ventured to look into the face
of her son nor speak with him. Pray tell
me, master, how she may know it is I. So
I spoke, and straightway he gave me his
answer: 'An easy saying will I tell thee
and fix it in thy heart : whomsoever of those
who are dead and gone thou lettest draw
nigh to the blood, he will speak the word
of truth ; whom thou dost begrudge it, he
will go back to his place.' So saying, the
spirit entered the house of Hades, the
spirit of great Teiresias, who had told the
decrees of the gods. But I kept my place
on the spot, till my mother came near and
drank the dark blood. Straightway she
knew me."

It is to Rohde and his famous book
"Psyche" [12] we owe it — a book which I
cannot help thinking has in other regards

set many simple things awry — that this service of blood has been recognized as a reminiscence or survival from a horizon of faith that has passed away. It lingered with other rites in the ceremonies of burial as mere form divorced from the earlier faith, which alone gave it meaning and which alone can give it now interpretation. It is a part of the old cult of souls, the feeding of the dead.

It was no cheerful place, this land of Hades where the shades abode. Slimy and wet were its paths, where the gloomy black poplar and willows grew, misty and murky was its air. The "asphodel moor" whither the souls were led by guide Hermes was not the green pastures. The pale, ghastly asphodel, blooming from its unsightly stem, haunts in the upper world, we know, the barren lands, and that was the part it played below. "Son of Laertes, seed of Zeus, Odysseus of many wiles, what seekest thou now, wretched man ? Why hast thou left the light of the sun to come here and look on the dead and see this joyless place?" [13]

Once, and once only, in Homer there is an allusion to the Elysian Fields where Rhadamanthys dwells, and where Menelaos, another kinsman of Zeus, will find a place of rest, "where is no snow, and no wintry storm, nor ever the torrent of rains, but ever the light-breathing zephyrs Oceanus sends from the west with cooling for men." But this, like the later refuge in the blessed islands, is only for here and there one of the great ones of this earth, such as are really of the kin of gods, and it was indeed, as such, a reminiscence of the old hero-worship, now for a time in abeyance, but to revive again in a reinvigorated Hellas.

For men after the flesh, the future life offers prospect neither of bliss nor of punishment. The passage, Odyssey XI. 566–631, which tells of the punishments of Tityos, Tantalos, Sisyphos, has been unmistakably identified by Wilamowitz-Moellendorff [14] as the product of a much later period, the times of Solon and Peisistratos, and infused with a spirit and with ideas for which Homeric life had no place.

For Homer's men, there was no hope for a future life in which action and personality were continued with values derived and transplanted from the world of sunlight and sense. Hades was a dreary land of banishment, where there was no trial or joy, nothing to risk and nothing to achieve. All this belonged to the life under the blessed sunlight, and when that closed, the mission of personality was at an end. The earlier faith had found its solace in the continuation of personal life through the family and the tribe, as symbolized in the continued sacrifices for the dead. Homeric thought while living still under the shadow of the tribal idea had lost in large measure its consolation, and could content itself only with recognition of the harsh inevitable.

Homer stands at the end, not the beginning of an order of life, civilization, and thought. His voice is the swan's song of an order that like all, both men and communities, which have lost, before or since, the power to trust and hope, was going down the ways of death. It told the tales of a mighty world whose record is left in the walls and art and treasure of Mykenai, Tiryns, Orchomenos, and told them in a guise of thought and speech peculiar to the old Ionian [16] tribal aristocracy, itself doomed, in its materialism and its lifeless adherence, to the forms without the spirit of the old, to extinction and death. Between Homer and the new Hellenic life, that found its centre in the Athens of Peisistratos and Perikles, there is a deep gulf fixed, and across it come only the words of Homer and the thud of the rhapsode's foot. But it is this gulf which made Homer's words the message from another world, and transformed the lays to a sacred book.

In the period between 750 and 600 B. C. Greece passed through a change that made it new from the foundations. It was the period of the transition from mediæval to classical Greece. The phenomenally rapid colonial expansion of the century from 750 to 650 B. C. marks the occasion, and to a large extent the cause. Within this century, prosperous mercantile colonies were formed along the coasts of the Euxine, the Ægean, the Mediterranean from Kolchis and the Crimea at the east to Cumæ and Marseilles on the west. Through the contrast with peoples of other race and tongue, the Greek people of many tribes and cities awoke to a consciousness of national unity, and the Greater Greece was born, named with the new name Hellas.

Trade with the colonies, and through the colonies with distant inland populations, burst into sudden vigor. Everywhere the Phœnician trader yielded to the Greek. Industries rapidly developed to supply the demands of trade. The smith, the cutler, the potter, the weaver, the dyer, the wheelwright, the shoemaker, and the shipbuilder, all were spurred to their utmost to supply the demands of the new export trade.

The demand for labor brought in the slave, a new element. Thus far Greece had known only the serf. Wealth poured into the land, luxury increased, the demands of life became greater and more diversified. The coinage of money, just begun, rapidly extended. Barter and local exchanges gave way to the money standard. Prices were no longer fixed by local conditions, but the remotest villages became part of the economic world at large.

Men flocked from the farms and pastures into the cities. The new wealth came often into the hands of others than the old nobility. Timocracy for a time displaced aristocracy. The new population of the mercantile and manufacturing centres, confused of merchants, tradesmen, manufacturers, and laborers, sundered from their old social and political ties, could no longer respect the traditional usages and classifications of tribal aristocratic institutions, which in the undisturbed life of the home and the village had never been questioned.

The old law and the old methods of administering justice no longer suffice. The new conditions demand one law for all, nobleman and laborer, and a court maintained by the state, and they demand that the caprice of the judge shall be limited by definite written statutes. Hence appear at this time all over Greece the great codifiers, Zaleukos the Locrian, Charondas of Katana, Pheidon of Corinth, Pittakos of Mitylene, Dracon, then Solon, in Athens.

In the political life, too, the old sacks would not do for the new wine. The old ruling class admits to its ranks here and there the holders of the new wealth and so compromises with the new situation, but the *tiers état*, the *demos*, pushes for a hearing, and the assembly (or *ekklesia*) gradually asserts its claim to be the state. In the rapid shifting of conditions political and economic, it was the peasant and the country squire who suffered most, but as is always the case when economic and social dislodgments such as this occur in the history of a people, discontent muttered on every hand. Discontent and joy are both the legitimate children of opportunity.

The breaking of the traditional moulds in which the old tribal life was set had released the individual from bondage to the destiny of that group into which he was born, and given him the opportunity, and thrown upon him the responsibility of a man. He became the bearer of his own destiny. With the rise of individualism, culture, thought, literature, institutions, and life hastened in widely branching differentiation to assume the many-sided type that sets the Greece of the sixth and following centuries in such marked contrast to the plain naïve monotony of its earlier days; for Greece had then passed out of childhood into the years of discretion and manhood.

The rapid change of attitude which had thus passed over the Greek people in respect to the world of politics, of society, of justice, of economics, could not fail to seek its expression in terms of the greater world of ultimate destiny and purpose. The individualism which had received in the marts equal opportunity, and had demanded of the courts equal justice, and was demanding of the state equal hearing, and which in life carried the burden of its own responsibility, could no longer be satisfied before the oracles of religion with a destiny that in arbitrary violence robbed personality of its fulfillment or merged its fate and its hope in the fate of the clan or the race.

The period with which we have been dealing marked the rise, and the following or sixth century the full development, of the Greek faith in personal immortality. From the seventh century on, new elements and new states, Corinth and Ægina, Megara and Sparta and Thebes, later Athens, came to the front in Greek affairs.

The civilization localized in the eastern hem of Greek life, that which Homer represents, and which bears the name of Ionian, burned itself out with luxury and material-

ism in the exuberance of its precocious
bloom. From the sturdy mountain peoples
of central Hellas, who had thus far remained in the background, and in their isolation from the culture of the Ægean had
preserved the old standards of simplicity
and the old usages of religion, came a fresh
infusion of Hellenic blood, new aggressive
vigor, and above all a sturdier faith. It was
preëminently the Dorian elements which
lent to this second wave of the Greek tide
its strength and mass. As it advanced
into eastern Greece, it took on the color
of the Eastern culture, but its life-strength
was the primitive old Greek spirit.

Everywhere the old simplicity of the
earlier Greek religion revived and became
the standard; indeed, with these peoples
themselves it had never flagged nor failed.
Soul-worship in all its various forms, offerings for the dead, the household gods, the
gods of clans, institutions like the pryta-
neion table as a feast with the gods of the
state, hero-worship, the worship of cave

spirits and mountain spirits, consultation of spirits and oracles, in all these and many other forms emerged, and emerged not from long sleep, but from long concealment.

While the old soul-worship offered a soil upon which a new vision and assurance of the mission and fate of the soul beyond the grave might arise, it could not in itself afford that vision or satisfy the newborn craving of men. It dealt only with the relations of the living to the dead, not with those of the living to their own future estate. Men wanted some knowledge of what they were themselves to be and do in the other life, and not merely to be occupied with conciliating the attitude of the spirits toward this life. That they should live after death, this they knew; no form of Greek faith had ever implied or taught anything else; no Greek of the folk had ever thought anything else; but *how* they were to live, that was what the individual in his consciousness of a personality possessing worth, meaning, and responsibility, desired to know.   To this desire the Mysteries of Eleusis gave answer first.

In the isolation of the Thriasian plain had been maintained at Eleusis, time out of mind, the peculiar cult of the earth-goddess Demeter.   Something had invested its strange rites with an unusual sanctity, but still its repute, like the membership in its guild, remained until near the end of the seventh century well-nigh restricted to the immediate locality.   It was a local institution, owned and controlled by a few great families of the parish.

After the union of Eleusis and Attika, however, and the reception of the cult under the protection and guarantee of the state, an entirely new and larger career was opened, especially when Peisistratos, as the tribune of the people, reformed and broadened the organization of the worship so as to open it to universal use and make it worthy of the state.

So it became, in contrast to the cults of phratry and clan, in which membership was determined by birth, an eminently democratic and popular association. No one was excluded, whatever his city or tribe. Citizens and metics, men and women, slaves and children, all were admitted. It was as individuals that they came to be cleansed, and to gain the assurances of future blessing, which the mysteries had to give, and so no wonder that it was the sixth century, the century of the awakened individualism, in which the mysteries acquired their unique popularity.

No one of the thousands initiated to the rites has ever betrayed their much debated secret. But they must, we can be certain, have offered something which answered to the quest of the times. "Blessed is he," says Pindar, [16] "who having seen these rites goeth under the earth. He knoweth the end of life, he knoweth too its god-disposed beginning." So Sophocles: [17] "Thrice happy they among mortals who depart into Hades after their eyes have seen these rites; yea, for them alone is there a life ; for other men all there is ill ;" and Plato in the Phædo :[18] "The founders of the mysteries would appear to have had a real meaning, and were not talking nonsense, when they intimated in a figure long ago, that he who passes unsanctified and uninitiated into the world below will lie in a slough, but that he who arrives there after initiation and purification will dwell with the gods," and in the Frogs Aristophanes lightens the gloom of the nether world with the song of the initiates, [19] who now dance in veritable flowery fields, — the song ending with the words : " We alone have the sun and its gladsome light, we who have taken the sacred vow, and have lived a life in the fear of god toward stranger and toward friend."

The testimony of all antiquity to the inspiring and uplifting influence of the mysteries is impressively unanimous. No voice is raised in criticism. Wherein lay their influence and convincing power we can only surmise from the sum of allusion. It certainly was not conveyed through doctrine or creed, argument or exhortation, but rather through some form of drama in which the loss and the resurrection of Persephone was the central event, and which like the Christian drama of the mass,[20] quickening the dormant faith, offered to the beholder some suggestion of a definite state and condition of future existence. No one seems to have questioned the validity or authority of the assurance that the initiated, and they alone, should find peace. They who saw knew, and they who knew must needs attain. It was no question of authority. They believed gladly, because constrained by their yearning to believe. The faith and its authority were within themselves.

Among the reforms of the Eleusinian worship, which in the sixth century virtually made the cult anew, and gave it its universally human form, and which all tend to attach themselves to the sponsorship of

Peisistratos, there is one which is almost certainly his work, and which apparently more than any other thing served to give the Mysteries their distinctive character. This was the introduction of the youth Iakchos and his worship into the family and bond of Demeter and Persephone. Most frequently the shifting myths represent him as son of Zeus and Persephone, rescued from the slaughter of the Titans to a new resurrection life. Sometimes he is a son of Demeter, sometimes of Dionysos, again he seems merely a shadow of Dionysos himself, but whatever he was, certain it is that his character and spirit was entirely the product of the Dionysos worship as shapen into the mystic forms of the Orphic theology. He was unmistakably the child Dionysos permanently separated and differentiated out of the whole story of Dionysos and made a distinct type by himself. Demeter searching in the darkness for her child that was lost — symbol of the seed-corn buried in the earth, offered a ready analogy

to the fostering love and care with which
the Mænad nurses tended the babe of Nysa,
— the springing vegetation of the new beginning year. Though it has been questioned — I think on insufficient grounds —
that the legend of Demeter and Persephone
has its source in the alternate disappearance
and reappearance of the grain, it cannot be
doubted that it came to be interpreted
in connection with that phenomenon and
received much of its character from the
analogy. In the cult of Dionysos-Iakchos,
however, resided from the beginning a direct
meaning for the experience of the individual human life, and it was through this
type of Iakchos that the mystery of Persephone's return was given its relation and
application to the resurrection hope of hu-
manity. The mysteries, in other words,
were made what they were by the ingraft-
ing of the Dionysos spirit.

The rise of Dionysos worship is the most
important single phenomenon in the history
of Greek religion. Unknown to the Ioni-

ans of Homer's day except as a local or a
stranger's worship, and having no place
within the Olympian circle, it arose from
its obscurity, and coming out from the
mountains and from the villages of pea-
sants, with the fresh flood of life that the
seventh century brought into eastern
Greece, it swept into city and state as the
Salvation Army of the *tiers état*, and in de-
fiance of all the opposition of the staid con-
servatives and of the aristocrats, who, cling-
ing to the old local and private worships,
would hear nothing of Demeter or Dionysos, it forced its way into public and official
recognition preëminently in Attika, dominated the popular interest, infused a new
life into the dead formalism of religion,
quickened and energized the entire intellectual and spiritual life of Greece to the
very finger tips.   It was the religion of
enthusiasm.

Its primitive form we know in outline
from the practices observed among the
Thracians, who like their brother Phrygi-

ans were distinguished as its devotees, and through whom indirectly the worship may well have found introduction into Greece, but usages and a belief in general analogous, and resting upon the same general attitude toward nature, are found widely scattered among European peoples.

A primitive belief that regards the life and death of vegetation after the analogies of human life, attributes the withering winter and the revival of spring to the departure and return, or the slumbering and reawakening, of the psyches or spirits whose reunion with matter all life consists. The spirits or *daimones* of the vegetation which has slumbered through the winter must needs be wakened or recalled in spring. In the wild dances and cries of those who act the life of the spirits they wish to recall, the bacchanal ecstasies have probably their root ; the blood of the torn victim which the mænad scatters over the ground is then a reminiscence of the blood which feeds the spirits and brings them to consciousness and activity; the mænad who devours the raw flesh and drinks the blood is herself inspired to the ecstasy which represents the revived and restored life; the satyrs who followed in the *thiasos* of Dionysos are in their first signification, if this all be true, mere embodiments of the *daimones* of vegetation conceived in the form of the victim through whose death they come to life, and following in the train of their lord Dionysos himself, who is Zagreus, the firstfruits of the resurrection. The limitation of his festivals to the period between the winter solstice, as the primitive Christmas, and the vernal equinox, as the primitive Easter, and his occupation of the Delphic shrine during the winter months while Apollo withdrew, would also conform to this explanation of the cult as involving the nurture and revival of the vegetation spirits.

But whether this be or be not the native source of the bacchanal rites, certain it is that their central feature from the earliest obtainable evidence is the " ecstasy " of the *orgia.* In many different forms among people of various civilization there appear ever and anon these practices whereby with different means the body is benumbed or otherwise brought into apparent subjection and annulment in order that the soul may wander in realms other than those of its every-day experience, and commune with spirits outside of and above the known. The reiterated cadences of music, the rhythm of the dance, the repetition of words, continued swaying or whirling of the body, the influences of narcotics or stimulants, are all used to produce in most various types, from that of the Indian medicine man to that of the Mahomedan dervish, these superpersonal states whereby one thinks to lose himself in union with the spirit world.

Though profoundly tempered from its primitive crudity in the atmosphere of Greece, and particularly in the sobering atmosphere of Attika, the holy madness of the Dionysos revels was in genesis and in spirit one and the same with them all.

Except as we appreciate this, we cannot understand the various outgrowths and influences of the Dionysiac religion, nor indeed that religion itself.

Even the drama, choicest of its products, and impersonation, upon which it depends for its existence, arise out of the Dionysiac effort to break loose from one life and live another. That which was at the beginning the charm of the drama, and has been, so far as it is true to itself, ever since, is its power to release those who behold it for a little while from the burden and inthrallment of the commonplace, workaday life, and bathe their wearied souls in dreams.

This is the very heart of Dionysos, and this, too, is his claim to control of the fruit of the vine. But his relation to the vine is no more than an incident. His mission is to lift men out of themselves and by bringing them into communion and association with that above and without them, to which they are unwittingly akin, and which is nobler, higher, and purer than they, to purge and renew them. He is the god of the cleansing in the ideal. As such Thebes, sunk in her pollution, calls upon him by the lips of the Sophoclean chorus to " come with cleansing foot over the slopes of Parnassos or over the moaning strait." [21]

His faith lay hard by the gate of mysticism, and men entered abundantly in. In Southern Italy, Sicily, and Attika, there arose during the sixth century the strange apparition of the Orphic theology. With its doctrine of the body as a prison house and of the soul as akin to God, of the long toil of liberation, and the devious way to reunion with its own, and the " wheel of births," it is a strange phenomenon indeed, and has tempted men to dream of some mysterious channel of Eastern influence, connecting, despite chronology, even with Buddha, which should explain this and Pythagoras as well.[22] But sharp as the contrast is with the traditional mood of Hellenic faith, both Orphism and Pythagoras are the products unmistakably and directly

of Dionysos. The Orphic religion is merely
a speculative theology of the Dionysiac
faith, confused with weird fancies and
popular superstition, and cast in poetic
mould, — that and nothing more.

Between the essential Pantheism of Indian thought and the mystical Idealism
involved in that feature of Greek thought
we are now discussing, there was in reality
no highway.   To the one the All is the
god ; the visible world of material is his
unfolding; there is from it no escape ; weal
is found in submission and accord.   To the
other the material things of sense are the
soul's ball and chain; the divine has cre-
ated them, but is not *in* them and they are
not *of* him ; weal is found in liberation and
flight.   The Dionysiac "way of salvation"
is the way of liberation and cleansing.   The
soul is in essence divine.   Because of its
sin it is shut off in the world of body
and matter.   The body is a prison.

Now and again in ecstatic vision the god-
born soul escapes from its duress, realizes

its higher being and mission, and revels in communion with its own. How to be rid forever of the ball and chain, how to turn the brief vision into a continuous life — that is the Dionysiac problem of salvation. Death will not accomplish it. Through the long circuit of births the soul must toil on, freeing itself more and more from the dross, until at the distant goal, "rescued from misery it breathes free at last."

In the recipe for cleansing and liberation, mortification of the body and moral asceticism found small place, or none at all. The question of morals [23] was for that matter in no wise involved. It was, if we may so term it, a metaphysical salvation, not a moral one, that men were seeking. The means of rescue, too, which was proposed, was positive, not negative, — *the expulsive power of the new insight*, we might name it, or better, the *uplifting power of the new insight*.

The force and influence of this new departure in the life of Greece did not exhaust itself in religious fervors. It laid hold upon all the thought of men and gave shape even to the forming moulds of philosophic reflection. Without Dionysos and Orphism there could have been, for instance, no Plato. Plato's philosophy builds on a faith, and that faith is Dionysism. Everywhere in his thinking[24] religion gleams through the thin gauze of philosophic form, and except his system be understood as a religion and as a part of the history of Greek religion, it yields no self-consistent interpretation, and is not intelligible either in its whence or whither. The things many and various he has to tell about the Ideas refuse to take orderly place and position in a doctrine of logical realism such as metaphysics teaches, but are satisfied all in a doctrine of spirituality and the higher life, such as poetry and religion can preach.

The universe which Plato feels is in substance the universe which the Dionysos enthusiasms presuppose. There is a world of the outward and material, ever shifting, unsteady, perishable, behind it is a world of

the unchanging norm, the essential purpose, the supreme reality. To the former
belongs the body, to the latter by nature
and source the soul. This mortal life is an
entanglement of the soul in the meshes of
the material. Still, through the perverting
and obscuring medium of that which enfolds
it the soul catches glimpses of the true,
and gathers intimations of its own kinship
with the ideal and the abiding. All the
Platonic arguments for the immortality of
the soul, in the Phædrus, in the Republic,[25]
in the Phædo, diverse as they seem, unite
as being merely various ways or devices
for setting forth a central faith whose first
inspiration had come from the Dionysos cult.

The influence of Eleusis and of Dionysos
covers all the latter day of Hellenic life,
but peculiarly strong is it written upon
the thought and in the literature of the
closing years of the sixth century and of
the greater portions of the fifth. The sixth
century marked a period of genuine religious revival, — not a revival merely of ob-

servances and rites, but a stirring of the
personal interest in matters of faith and
personal destiny that approaches the development of what we know as personal religion. We miss, to be sure, from our point
of view, the firm outlines of a formulated
theologic faith concerning personal relation
to the eternal, such as we are wont to iden-
tify with personal religion ; but men were
thinking in terms of individual responsibility, and forms of theology distinct from
the state and tribal types were emerging
and were preparing the way for the ration-
alism of which Euripides stands in literature as the early exponent.

Expressions concerning the life after
death, however much they might cling to
the traditional moulds of the old-time, or to
what we may call the Homeric, faith regard-
ing the geography of Hades, showed, as
contrasted with the Homeric view, a radi-
cal change in the conception of the life
itself. Thus Pindar : [26]

" Victory setteth free the essayer from

the struggle's griefs, yea, and the wealth that a noble nature hath made glorious bringeth power for this and that, putting into the heart of man a deep and eager mood, a star far seen, a light wherein a man shall trust, if but the holder thereof knoweth the things that shall be, how that of all who die the guilty souls pay penalty, for all the sins sinned in this realm of Zeus One judgeth under earth, pronouncing sentence by unloved constraint.

"But evenly ever in sunlight night and day an unlaborious life the good receive, neither with violent hand vex they the earth nor the waters of the sea, in that new world ; but with the honored of the gods, whosoever had pleasure in keeping of oaths, they possess a tearless life ; but the other part suffer pain too dire to look upon.

" Then whosoever have been of good courage to the abiding steadfast thrice on either side of death, and have refrained their souls from all iniquity, travel the road of Zeus unto the tower of Kronos ; there

around the islands of the blest the ocean
breezes blow, and golden flowers are glow-
ing, some from the land on trees of splen-
dor, and some the water feedeth, with
wreaths whereof they entwine their hands :
So ordereth Rhadamanthos' just decree,
whom at his own right hand hath ever the
father Kronos, husband of Rhea, throned
above all worlds."

Similarly in the following fragments of
dirges : —

"For them shineth below the strength
of the sun while in our world it is night,
and the space of crimson-flowered meadows
before their city is full of the shade of
frankincense trees, and of fruits of gold.
And some in horses, and in bodily feats, and
some in dice, and some in harp-playing
have delight ; and among them thriveth all
fair-flowered bliss ; and fragrance streameth
ever through the lovely land, as they
mingle incense of every kind upon the
altars of the gods.[27]

"By happy lot travel all unto an end that

giveth them rest from toils. And the body indeed is subject unto the great power of death, but there remaineth yet alive a shadow of the life; for this only is from the gods ; and while the limbs stir, it sleepeth, but unto sleepers in dreams discovereth oftentimes the judgment that draweth nigh for sorrow or for joy." [28]

Most significant here, as betraying how fully Pindar's thought shaped itself in Dionysiac or Orphic moulds, are the expressions "this only is from the gods," and "while the limbs stir, it sleepeth." The real existence of the soul as the divine element of man's life is the existence freed from the constraint of the body which dulls it and prevents it from seeing and knowing clearly. This is Paul's " Now we see in a mirror darkly."

Another more distinctively Orphic touch is involved in a third fragment : "But from whomsoever Persephone accepteth atonement for an ancient woe, their souls unto the light of the sun above she sendeth

back again in the ninth year. And from
those souls spring noble kings, and men
swift and strong and in wisdom very great:
and through the after-time they are called
holy heroes among men." [29]

Sophocles represents his Antigone as act-
ing in this present world of transitory and
superficial law in respect for the "unwrit-
ten, irrefragable ordinances of the gods," [30]
which "not for to-day alone and for yester-
day but forever have their life, — and no
man knoweth whence they are." [31]   These
laws are the laws of Hades as the great
other, outer world of the eternal, and they
govern the judgments at the bar of Diké,
who "dwells with the nether gods." In defi-
ance of temporal law she performs the
burial rites of her brother: "Fair thing it
is for me in doing this to die; dear shall I
lie with him my dear one, having wrought
a pious crime; for longer is the time that I
must please the ones below than those up
here; since there forever shall I lie." [32]   In
obeying the laws of the nether kingdom

she counts herself already its subject and its citizen; such she has become that she may minister unto those of her kindred who dwell within it. Her sister Ismene, who in fear of the laws of the upper world has withheld her aid, she counts as of this world. "Thou art alive, but my soul long since passed into death, to minister unto those who are dead." [33]

It is in the light of this sense for a continuance of personal ties beyond the grave, that the Attic sepulchral monuments, with their peaceful scenes of family reunion and association, must find their rightful interpretation. It remained now for Plato, in harmony with this newly quickened conception of a real personal continuance after death and continuance in a life bearing relations to the life on earth, to offer the first philosophic argument for the immortality of the soul.

The chirping psyches of Homer's nether world were mere phantom apologies to a stolid, helpless belief in continuance; the offerings to the dead practised among the early non-Homeric Greeks were a tribute to the idea of tribal and family unity. This was all that the older faith of the Greeks could offer.

With Dionysos, however, there came into Greek religion and thought a new element, an utterly new point of view. He taught his followers to know that the inner life of man, the soul, is of like substance with the gods, and that it may commune with the divine. Before the days of his revelation there had been between the generations of mortal men, who fell like the generations of leaves, and the undying gods whose food is ambrosia and whose drink nectar, a gulf fixed deep and impassable. After his revelation the soul was divine and might claim an immortality like to that of the gods.

Dionysos had waited long in the vales of Nysa and Parnassos, buried like the uncut gem in crude and uncouth guise, but when the need and desire of men sought after him he came to help.

A human hand, lifting its grasp toward immortality, stands a mute witness to a consciousness arising in the single human soul that it has a meaning in itself, that it has a purpose and a mission of its own, that it holds direct account with the heart of the world, and of a world to whose peerage it belongs and with whose plan and reason it has rights and a hearing.

The faiths of men are quoted under various names and are set forth in various articles, but we may not be confused thereby, for men are men ; control of nature has grown stronger and history longer since the day when Greece first frankly and straight looked nature and life in the face, but man himself stays much the same, — given the same conditions, the plain touch of need makes all the centuries kin.

If in the throb of Dionysos' passion men seem to gain an insight into the spiritual harmonies of nature, and intimations of their own potential kinship with the divine, which cold reason and dull sense had not availed to give, it was still dim, groping vision ; but yet the face was set thither, where, in a later day, — a day for which Greece and Dionysos prepared, — men learned through the Convincing Love to know and live the eternity within them.

NOTES

NOTE 1, page 8.

J. Lippert: *Die Religionen der europäischen Culturvölker in ihrem geschichtlichen Ursprunge,* Berlin, 1881; E. Rohde: *Psyche; Seelencult und Unsterblichkeitsglaube unter den Griechen,* 2d ed., Freiburg, 1898, pp. 1 ff; De Coulanges: *The Ancient City,* Eng. transl. pp. 28 ff.

NOTE 2, page 8.

It certainly is unsafe to speak of an Indo-European religion without making some explanation of what may be meant by such a term, and what may be supposed to be known or knowable concerning such a subject. It is no longer to be assumed that all the peoples who appear in history, possessed of an Indo-European tongue, are necessarily in all their make-up descendants of what is called the Indo-European race. The presumption is against it, and so is the ethnological evidence. There was certainly an Indo-European language; therefore there was once a people who spoke it. The extension of the language through conquest — the conquered peoples gradually accepting the language of the conquerors — is doubtless a more important point of view than that of its extension by migration and increase of the racial stock. The breaking up into distinct languages must, it seems likely, be accounted for in large measure through the influence of the alien tongues of the elements absorbed. The Greeks, for instance, were evidently not of one race; *i. e.*, those who at the beginning of history were speakers of Greek, were to a large extent representatives of the primitive populations inhabiting Greece before the Indo-European northmen entered the land. The fair-haired, blue-eyed people were, in the earliest times, a superior class, distinguished from the dark-complexioned peoples who gradually absorbed the former, so far as physiological type was concerned.

The early hopes of the science of comparative religion, as represented by Kuhn and Max Müller, were based on a false confidence in the methods of comparative philology. It was expected that comparison of the various cults of the different Indo-European peoples would yield a restoration of the primitive proethnic cults, just as the comparison of word-forms yielded a possible restoration of the primitive Indo-European vocabulary. The result has defeated these hopes. Comparison fails to discover any considerable number either of names of deities, or of fixed outlines of divine personalities, or of systematic forms of belief. The organization of the different religions of the so-called Indo-European peoples is evidently in the main their own separate achievement. Whether this has been brought about through the influence of the local beliefs and cults of the absorbed populations, or developed directly out of the materials of a primitive Indo-European religion, has not yet proved determinable, but many facts point in the direction of the former view. When we speak, therefore, of a proethnic Indo-European religion, we cannot refer to a definite system of personified powers, but only to a general attitude in character of belief which the broadest comparison of the different religions shows to be present as a basis in all of them.

NOTE 3, page 12.

When we venture to refer to a præ-Homeric religion, it must be understood that we are here beyond the range of documentary evidence. Inferences from the known facts of later Greek religion, from the facts of other Indo-European religions, and from the scanty and as yet imperfectly interpreted remains of Mycenæan civilization constitute our only guidance. The altar-pit in the courtyard at Tiryns, and the evidence that the

Mycenæan tombs were virtually houses of the dead, to which the altar-pits above them brought the blood-offering and food for the departed, join with the prior facts of Indo-European religion and the later facts of historic Greek religion to confirm a tolerably certain line of historical development.

NOTE 4, page 12.

"Wir haben hinreichenden Grund, einen Seelen-cult, eine Verehrung des im Menschen selbst ver-borgen lebenden, nach dessen Tode zu selbstän-digem Dasein ausscheidenden Geisterwesens auch in Griechenland, wie wohl überall auf Erden, unter den ältesten Bethätigungen der Religion zu ver-muthen. Lange vor Homer hat der Seelencult in den Grabgewölben zu Mykene und an anderen Stätten ältester Cultur sich seine Heiligthümer erbaut." E. Rohde : *Die Religion der Griechen*, Rectoratsrede, Heidelberg, 1894. Except as this fundamental point, established by the brilliant ar-gument of Rohde in his *Psyche*, is accepted, no in-telligible connection between the Greek faiths of different times and places is possible, — and what is more, no connection of the Greek faith with the Indo-European that lay behind it.

NOTE 5, page 12.

H. Oldenberg : *Die Religion des Veda*, pp. 543 ff.

NOTE 6, page 13.

See *Odyssey* XI. 220 ff.

NOTE 7, page 14.

Rohde (*Psyche*, pp. 27 ff.) connects the Homeric freedom from dreamed-of ghosts with the practice of cremation. He even attributes the introduction of the practice to a desire to be rid of the spirits through help of the "cleansing force of fire." The primitive notion that the spirits haunted the place where the body remained, and hung about the body itself, would naturally lead to the belief that the total destruction of the body would remove this lure to the spirits and take from them the way of approach to the homes of the living. The difficulty with Rohde's suggestion is, however, that it takes no account of the fact that cremation appears as an institution so widespread among Indo-European peoples as to demand almost certainly a place among primitive Indo-European usages.

It may have been in vogue only among certain tribes, or have been employed at certain times, as in war or during absence from home, or for certain classes, as the kings and chieftains ; no solution of the strange problem has yet been found, but surely we are not justified in connecting a new departure in faith, such as Rohde thinks the Homeric liberation from the soul-cults represents, with a practice which is old and not new. The history of cremation in its connection with the primitive beliefs concerning immortality is a subject demanding a much more careful and comprehensive investigation than has yet been accorded it. Facts in abundance are known concerning the usages of various times and peoples, but no principle yet discovered has served to give these facts an intelligent connection.

NOTE 8, page 15.
See *Iliad* XXIII. 66 ff.

NOTE 9, page 15.
Teiresias the seer alone an exception.

NOTE 10, page 17.
See *Odyssey* XXIV. 1 ff.

NOTE 11, page 17.
See *Odyssey* XI. 24 ff.

NOTE 12, page 18.
E. Rohde: *Psyche; Seelencult und Unsterblichkeitsglaube unter den Griechen*, 2d ed., Freiburg, 1898.

NOTE 13, page 20.
See *Odyssey* XI. 92 ff (Teiresias to Odysseus).

NOTE 14, page 20.

See *Homerische Untersuchungen*, 199 ff.

NOTE 15, page 22.

The fundamental materials of the Homeric epic are undoubtedly Æolic or North Greek in their source. The language alone is enough to betray this. Æolic forms of the language have been preserved in the midst of the prevailing Ionic wherever the Ionic equivalents would not suit the metrical necessities. This concerns, however, only the formation of the peculiar, half-artificial idiom which finally became the rhapsodic fashion of speech. The civilization to which the songs as we have them were addressed was that of the old Ionic life of the central coast of Asia Minor, and in the current ideas of this civilization we must believe the setting of the stories was moulded. Homer therefore represents preëminently the life and atmosphere of the early Ionia in the period which antedates the rise of extensive commerce and the sending out of the commercial colonies. That which gave Homer so soon in the ears of the succeeding generations the ring of the remote and the heroic was the rapid shifting in scene and conditions introduced by the ninth and the eighth centuries. Life changed from the tribal-patriarchal to the urban-commercial basis. Coupled with this was the circumstance that the memories of the old Achæan civilization which had yielded the first materials of the stories were rapidly dulled into remote traditions by the disappearance of the states and the peoples that had carried the burden of this civilization. This disappearance is in some way connected with the emergence of the Dorians in eastern Greece. Here we confront the problem of the " Dorian Migrations."

NOTE 16, page 31.

Pindar: Bergk, *Poet. Lyr. Fragm.*, 137.

NOTE 17, page 31.

Sophocles : *Fragm.*, 719 (Dind.).

NOTE 18, page 32.

Plato : *Phædo*, p. 69 (transl. Jowett).

NOTE 19, page 32.

" Let us hasten — let us fly —
Where the lovely meadows lie;
Where the living waters flow ;
Where the roses bloom and blow.
Heirs of immortality.
Segregated, safe and pure,
Easy, sorrowless, secure ;
Since our earthly course is run,
We behold a brighter sun.

Holy lives — a holy vow —
Such rewards await them now."
Frere's transl. of Aristophanes, *Frogs*, 448–459.

NOTE 20, page 33.

For a most illumining view of the influence of
the mysteries upon the early Christian ritual, see
E. Hatch : *The Influence of Greek Ideas and Usages
upon the Christian Church.* Hibbert Lectures, 1888.
Lect. X. pp. 281 ff.

NOTE 21, page 41.

Sophocles : *Antigone*, 1143–45.

NOTE 22, page 41.

For the most explicit statement and discussion
of such views, see, *e. g.*, Leopold von Schroeder:
Pythagoras und die Inder, Leipzig, 1884; Richard
Garbe : *The Connection between Indian and Greek
Philosophy.* An address delivered before the
Philol. Congress at Chicago, July, 1893 (*Monist*,
1894, p. 176 and following).

NOTE 23, page 43.

The Orphic theology has often been pronounced
un-Hellenic in character and tone. Those who
would find for it an Eastern or Egyptian origin
emphasize its supposed discord with Greek ideas.

Surely it would be a stranger and interloper if it
proposed to a Greek world an ethical reformation
based upon a code of morals. Nothing could have
been more un-Hellenic than that. But herein lies
the core of the misunderstanding. Orphism con-
tained no suggestion of moral reform, and its ecstasies no more proposed an influence upon conduct
or morals than the " blessed seasons " of a negro
revival meeting. If Orphism is non-Greek, then is
also the idealism of Plato, which in its religious
bearings is its offspring. Both are, however, profoundly Greek, and only reflect the all-pervading
dualism of the popular psychology. What was new
in Orphism and in its common basis Bacchism was
the element of enthusiasm, the *communion* with the
divine. It was the " evangelical " religion of Greece.

It may be cause for wonder that a religious movement of such freshness and vigor should apparently
have lost itself in the marshes, and have exercised
no more definite influence upon the thought of the
after-world. To this it can first of all be said that
the real extent of its influence may easily have been
underestimated. Orphism in its organized form
passed quickly out of sight in the fifth century, but
its fundamental idea as expressed in Bacchism was
absorbed into the common thought of Greece. It
must furthermore be noticed that it came as an
infusion into Greek religion at a time when this

religion by reason of shifting historical conditions was moving toward inevitable decline. Greek religion was a thing of the *polis*, the city built of the amalgamated tribes and clans. With the *polis* it stood, and with the fall of the *polis* as a unit of government it fell. Its gods were chief citizens of the *polis*, members honorary of the associated guilds. When a greater world of commerce, intercourse, manners, and ideas arose, in which the cities came more and more, in spite of all theory to the contrary, to be no more than nuclei of population, the city gods and the city religions did not arise to meet its need. Not even Olympus raised Zeus high enough to oversee the land. The allegiance of men gradually transferred itself from the *polis* to the empire as the greater state, — even when they knew it not, and even when the empire was scarcely more than a vision dimly discerned through the warring fragments of Alexander's state. This they personified in the heroic form of Alexander, son of Ammon, — the new Zeus; his successors became the emperors of Rome. Through them the ideal of a Holy Empire was transmitted to the afterworld. Through all this shifting of the scenes Bacchism in outward form of organization could not hold itself erect, but its spirit came ever more and more to be the thought of the world. The impulse it had awakened found to no slight extent its satisfaction in Christianity ; and, on the other hand, Paganism in its last struggle against the propaganda of the Cross, when it chose its fittest armor, chose that most like the weapons of its foe, — Neo-Platonism, the last expression of the Dionysos faith.

Note 24, page 44.

The essential tone of Plato's writing is admirably set forth in the following statement, — a statement, it should, however, be said in justice to the author, not intended to support any such theory of Plato's connection with Orphism and Dionysos worship as that presented in the text: "He transmits the final outcome of Greek culture to us in no quintessential distillation of abstract formulas, but in vivid dramatic pictures that make us actual participants in the spiritual intoxication, the Bacchic revelry of philosophy, as Alcibiades calls it, that accompanied the most intense, disinterested, and fruitful outburst of intellectual activity in the annals of mankind." Paul Shorey, *Plato*, in Libr. of World's Best Literature.

Note 25, page 45.

Republic, pp. 609, 610, presents a form of argument which has often been said (cf. Grote: *Plato*, II. p. 190) to be entirely distinct from the other Platonic arguments.

NOTE 26, page 46.
Pindar : *Olymp*. II. 95 ff. (transl. Myers).

NOTE 27, page 48.
Pindar : *Fragm. Thren.*, I. (transl. Myers).

NOTE 28, page 49.
Pindar : *Fragm. Thren.*, II. (transl. Myers).

NOTE 29, page 50.
Pindar : *Fragm. Thren.*, III. (transl. Myers).

NOTE 30, page 50.
Sophocles: *Antigone*, 454.

NOTE 31, page 50.
Sophocles: *Antigone*, 456 ff.

NOTE 32, page 50.
Sophocles: *Antigone*, 72 ff.

NOTE 33, page 51.
Sophocles : *Antigone*, 559 ff.

www.ingramcontent.com/pod-product-compliance
Lightning Source LLC
Chambersburg PA
CBHW020244090426
42735CB00010B/1831